THE DEATH PENALTY: A CRITICAL EXAMINATION OF CAPITAL PUNISHMENT IN MODERN SOCIETY

Muhammad Khalid Aziz Bari

This book is dedicated to all those affected by the death penalty, whether as victims, offenders, families, or advocates. It is a tribute to the courage and resilience of those who have worked tirelessly to promote justice, human rights, and the rule of law in the face of significant challenges and obstacles.
In particular, this book is dedicated to the memory of those who have been unjustly executed or wrongfully convicted and to their families and loved ones who continue to seek justice and accountability. May their struggles and sacrifices inspire us to work towards a more just and humane world where every life is valued and respected.

"Our lives begin to end the day we become silent about things that matter."

MARTIN LUTHER KING JR.

CONTENTS

INTRODUCTION

Capital punishment, or the death penalty, has been debated for centuries. Taking someone's life as a punishment for a crime is a controversial issue that raises questions about the nature of justice, the value of human life, and the state's role in enforcing laws. The death penalty is currently practised in many countries worldwide, although the number of countries that have abolished it has increased.

The use of the death penalty has a long history, with different societies and cultures adopting various forms of execution to punish crimes such as murder, treason, and other serious offences. While some communities have used execution to maintain order and deter potential criminals, others have seen it as a cruel punishment that violates the rights of the condemned.

The death penalty has become highly contentious in modern times, with advocates and opponents presenting arguments based on morality, justice, and practical considerations. Supporters argue that the death penalty is a crime deterrent and provides a sense of closure for victims' families. They also say that certain crimes are so heinous that they warrant the ultimate punishment. On the other hand, opponents of the death penalty argue that it violates human rights and that the risk of wrongful convictions is too high. They also point to evidence of racial and socioeconomic biases in applying the death penalty and argue that it is ineffective in preventing crime.

In light of these arguments, critically examining the death penalty's role in modern society is essential. This book aims to comprehensively analyze the death penalty, its history, its arguments for and against its use, and its impact on human rights and social justice. The book will also examine alternatives to the death penalty and consider how the criminal justice system can be reformed to ensure justice is served fairly and equitably.

The issue of capital punishment is complex and multifaceted, and many different factors must be considered when evaluating its use. For example, the legal frameworks governing the use of the death penalty vary widely across other countries and jurisdictions, and the methods of execution used can differ significantly. In addition, the cultural, social, and political contexts in which the death penalty is applied can dramatically impact its effectiveness and perceived legitimacy.

Furthermore, the issue of capital punishment raises critical ethical questions about the value of human life and the state's role in administering justice. Many opponents of the death penalty argue that taking a person's life as a punishment for a crime violates the fundamental human right to life. In contrast, supporters often say that certain crimes are so heinous that they warrant the ultimate punishment. These debates reflect broader philosophical questions about the nature of justice and the appropriate limits of state power.

In recent years, the use of the death penalty has become increasingly controversial, with many countries moving to abolish it because it is an outdated and ineffective form of punishment. This has led to a growing movement favouring alternatives to the death penalty, such as life imprisonment without parole, restorative justice, and rehabilitation programs. These alternatives are more effective at preventing crime and promoting social justice while respecting the accused's human rights.

In conclusion, the issue of capital punishment is complex and multifaceted, raising important questions about justice, human rights, and the state's role in administering discipline. This book aims to critically examine the death penalty in modern society, exploring its history, the arguments for and against its use, and its impact on human rights and social justice. By considering these issues in depth, it is hoped that readers will understand the complex ethical and social issues surrounding capital punishment and the need for alternatives that promote justice and respect for human rights.

PREFACE

This book is intended to critically examine capital punishment in modern society, exploring the history, arguments, and alternatives surrounding this complex issue. Drawing on a range of legal, social, and ethical perspectives, this book seeks to provide a comprehensive and nuanced understanding of the death penalty and its place in contemporary justice systems.

While I have done my best to present a balanced and evidence-based view of the death penalty, it is essential to acknowledge that this issue is deeply personal and often highly charged. Many people have strong feelings and beliefs about the death penalty based on their experiences, values, and perspectives. This book will contribute to a constructive and informed dialogue on this topic that respects diverse viewpoints and fosters mutual understanding and respect.

I want to express my gratitude to all those who have contributed to this book, including the many scholars, experts, and practitioners who have generously shared their insights and expertise. I would also like to thank the readers who have taken the time to engage with this critical issue and have played a vital role in shaping the ongoing conversation about the death penalty. I hope this book will provide a valuable resource for anyone seeking to understand the complexities of the death penalty and its impact on modern society. Whether you are a student, scholar, policy-maker, or concerned citizen, the insights and perspectives presented in this book will help inform and enrich your understanding of this critical issue.

PROLOGUE

On a cold and windy night in Huntsville, Texas, a man was led into a small, dimly lit room. He had spent the last 20 years on death row, convicted of a brutal murder that he maintained he did not commit. As he was strapped to the gurney and the lethal injection began to flow into his veins, he whispered a final prayer and closed his eyes.

The execution of this man was not an isolated incident. Around the world, thousands of people are executed each year, many of them for crimes that do not meet the international standards for the death penalty. While some countries have abolished the death penalty, others continue to use it to punish the most heinous crimes.

The use of the death penalty raises profound questions about justice, morality, and human rights. Is the death penalty an appropriate response to the most severe crimes, or is it a cruel and inhumane practice that violates the sanctity of life? Does the death penalty deter crime, or does it simply perpetuate a cycle of violence and retribution? These are complex and challenging questions that demand careful consideration and reflection.

This book explores the death penalty issues, drawing on various legal, social, and ethical perspectives. It is not intended to provide a definitive answer to whether the death penalty is right or wrong but rather to provide a comprehensive and nuanced understanding of the complexities of this issue.

Whether you are a staunch supporter of the death penalty or

a passionate opponent, I hope this book will challenge your assumptions, broaden your perspectives, and encourage you to engage in a thoughtful and informed dialogue about this critical issue. The stakes are high, and our decisions about the death penalty have far-reaching consequences for our societies, our values, and our shared humanity.

SUMMARY

Introduction

Capital punishment, also known as the death penalty, is one of the most controversial forms of punishment in modern society. While some argue that it serves as a necessary deterrent to crime, others believe it violates human rights and should be abolished. This book will examine the death penalty in modern society and critically evaluate its place in the criminal justice system.

Chapter 1: History of Capital Punishment

This chapter will explore the history of capital punishment from ancient times to the modern day. It will provide an overview of the various methods of execution used throughout history and examine the reasons behind their use. It will also discuss the evolution of the death penalty in different countries and how cultural, social, and political factors have influenced it.

Chapter 2: Arguments for and Against the Death Penalty

This chapter will explore the arguments for and against the death penalty. It will provide a detailed analysis of why some people support the death penalty, including its potential as a deterrent to crime and its ability to provide closure for victims' families. It will also examine why others oppose the death penalty, including concerns about wrongful convictions, potential bias and discrimination, and ethical considerations.

Chapter 3: The Death Penalty and Human Rights

This chapter will explore the issue of human rights regarding the death penalty. It will examine how the death penalty can be seen as a violation of human rights and discuss the international legal frameworks that govern the use of the death penalty. It will also examine how the death penalty has been used as a political repression tool and consider its ethical implications.

Chapter 4: The Death Penalty and Race

This chapter will examine how race and ethnicity have played a role in using the death penalty. It will explore the evidence of racial bias in the application of the death penalty and discuss how the death penalty has been used as a tool of oppression against minority groups. It will also examine how the death penalty has been used to perpetuate systemic racism in the criminal justice system.

Chapter 5: Alternatives to the Death Penalty

This chapter will explore the alternatives to the death penalty available in modern society. It will discuss the different forms of punishment that can replace the death penalty, including life imprisonment without parole, restorative justice, and rehabilitation programs. It will also examine these alternatives' potential benefits and drawbacks and consider their effectiveness in preventing crime.

Chapter 6: Conclusion

This chapter will summarise the key points discussed in the book and offer a conclusion on the death penalty in modern society. It will consider how the death penalty can be seen as a necessary tool of justice and a violation of human rights. It will also discuss the potential for reform and how the criminal justice system can be improved to ensure justice is served fairly and equitably.

CHAPTER 1:
HISTORY OF CAPITAL
PUNISHMENT

C apital punishment has a long and complex history spanning many societies and cultures. The death penalty can be traced back to ancient civilizations such as Babylon, China, and Egypt, where it was used as a punishment for murder, theft, and treason.

In ancient Rome, the use of the death penalty was widespread and often carried out in public. Executions were typically carried out using crucifixion, beheading, or burning at the stake and were often accompanied by public spectacles such as gladiator games or animal fights.

During the Middle Ages, the use of the death penalty continued to be widespread throughout Europe and was often used as a means of enforcing religious conformity. Heretics, witches, and other perceived threats to the established order were often executed gruesomely, such as being burned at the stake or being drawn and quartered.

The use of the death penalty in modern times can be traced back to the Enlightenment era when thinkers such as Cesare Beccaria argued that punishment should be proportionate to the crime committed and that the death penalty should only be used in the most extreme cases. This view was reflected in the legal codes of many European countries, which restricted the use of the death penalty to a small number of crimes, such as murder and treason.

In the United States, the death penalty dates back to colonial times, when it was used as a punishment for crimes such as witchcraft and piracy. Over time, the death penalty became more widespread, and by the mid-20th century, it was widely used throughout the country.

However, in recent decades, the use of the death penalty in the United States has become increasingly controversial, with many states abolishing it because it is an ineffective and inhumane form of punishment. In 1972, the U.S. Supreme Court temporarily suspended the use of the death penalty, ruling that its application was unconstitutional due to its arbitrary and discriminatory nature. The death penalty was reinstated in 1976, but many states have since abolished it or placed moratoriums on its use.

Today, the use of the death penalty remains highly controversial, with advocates and opponents presenting arguments based on morality, justice, and practical considerations. While some argue that the death penalty serves as a deterrent to crime and provides a sense of closure for victims' families, others say that it violates human rights and that the risk of wrongful convictions is too high. The debate over the use of the death penalty is likely to continue for many years as societies grapple with questions about the nature of justice and the appropriate limits of state power.

Despite its long history, the use of capital punishment remains a highly contentious issue worldwide. Many countries have abolished the death penalty entirely, while others continue to use it, often in very different ways. In some countries, such as Saudi Arabia and Iran, the death penalty is used extensively, with hundreds of executions yearly. In others, such as Japan and

Singapore, the death penalty is used more sparingly but remains part of the legal system.

One of the key criticisms of the death penalty is that it is often applied unfairly, with certain groups, such as minorities and the poor, disproportionately represented on death row. This can be due to various factors, including unequal access to legal representation and bias among judges and juries. In the United States, for example, studies have shown that African Americans and Latinos are more likely to be sentenced to death than white defendants, even when controlling for other factors, such as the severity of the crime.

Another essential criticism of the death penalty is that it is irreversible, meaning there is always the risk of executing an innocent person. This risk is heightened in countries where the legal system is flawed or corrupt and defendants may not have access to adequate legal representation or a fair trial. In recent years, several high-profile cases of wrongful convictions have led to increased scrutiny of the death penalty, with many questioning its continued use in light of these injustices.

Despite these criticisms, some argue that the death penalty is necessary for the most heinous crimes, such as murder and terrorism. Supporters of the death penalty often say that it provides a sense of justice for victims and their families and serves as a deterrent to would-be offenders. However, research on the effectiveness of the death penalty as a block is mixed, with some studies suggesting that it has little impact on crime rates.

In conclusion, the history of capital punishment is long and complex, with the death penalty evolving in response to changing societal norms and legal frameworks. While the death penalty remains in use in many countries worldwide, its continued usage is increasingly being questioned by critics who argue that it is an ineffective and unjust punishment. The debate over the use of the death penalty is likely to continue for many years as societies grapple with questions about the nature of justice and the appropriate limits of state power.

CHAPTER 2: ARGUMENTS FOR AND AGAINST THE DEATH PENALTY

T he use of the death penalty is one of the most contentious issues in criminal justice, with arguments on both sides based on morality, justice, and practical considerations. In this chapter, we will examine the main arguments for and against the use of the death penalty.

Arguments for the Death Penalty:

1. Deterrence: One of the most common arguments in favour of the death penalty is that it serves as a deterrent to crime. Proponents argue that the threat of being executed will discourage would-be offenders from committing serious crimes, such as murder.

2. Retribution: Another common argument favouring the death penalty is that it provides a sense of vindication for victims and their families. Supporters argue that those who commit heinous crimes, such as murder, deserve to be punished in the harshest way possible.

3. Public safety: Some proponents of the death penalty argue that it helps to protect society by permanently removing dangerous criminals from the streets. By executing those who commit the most serious crimes, such as serial killers or terrorists, the community is protected from the risk of future harm.

4. Justice: Finally, some supporters of the death penalty argue that it is the only just punishment for certain crimes. They say that some crimes, such as terrorism or mass murder, are so heinous that they deserve the ultimate death penalty.

Arguments Against the Death Penalty:

1. Human rights: Perhaps the most compelling argument against the death penalty is that it violates the fundamental human right to life. Many opponents of the death penalty argue that no one has the right to take another person's life, regardless of the circumstances.

2. Wrongful convictions: Another key argument against the death penalty is that it is irreversible, meaning there is always the risk of executing an innocent person. This risk is heightened in countries where the legal system is flawed or corrupt and defendants may not have access to adequate legal representation or a fair trial.

3. Racial and economic bias: Opponents of the death penalty argue that it is often applied unfairly, with certain groups, such as minorities and the poor, disproportionately represented on death row. This can be due to various factors, including unequal access to legal representation and bias among judges and juries.

4. Ineffectiveness: Finally, some opponents of the death penalty argue that it is ineffective. They point to studies that suggest that the death penalty has little or no impact on crime rates and say that alternative forms of

punishment, such as life imprisonment without parole, are more effective at deterring crime.

In conclusion, the arguments for and against the death penalty are complex and multifaceted. While some argue that the death penalty is necessary for the most heinous crimes, others say that it violates human rights and that the risk of wrongful convictions is too high. The debate over the use of the death penalty is likely to continue for many years as societies grapple with questions about the nature of justice and the appropriate limits of state power.

CHAPTER 3: THE DEATH PENALTY AND HUMAN RIGHTS

T he use of the death penalty has long been a contentious issue in human rights. The death penalty is seen by many as a violation of fundamental human rights, particularly the right to life. This chapter will examine the relationship between the death penalty and human rights and the international standards and norms that have emerged in response to this issue.

The Right to Life:

The right to life is a fundamental human right enshrined in many international human rights instruments, including the Universal Declaration of Human Rights, the International Covenant on Civil and Political Rights, and the European Convention on Human Rights. The death penalty is seen by many as a direct violation of this right, as it involves the state taking an individual's life.

International Standards and Norms:

Over the years, several international standards and norms have emerged in response to using the death penalty. In 1989, the

United Nations General Assembly adopted the Second Optional Protocol to the International Covenant on Civil and Political Rights, which called for abolishing the death penalty. Since then, several countries have ratified the protocol, signalling their commitment to abolishing capital punishment.

The Council of Europe has also strongly advocated for abolishing the death penalty and has worked to promote this goal through the European Convention on Human Rights. The Convention prohibits the death penalty, except in cases of war or imminent threat of war.

Human Rights Concerns:

Several human rights concerns arise in the context of the death penalty. One concern is the potential for wrongful convictions, which can result in the execution of innocent individuals. This risk is exceptionally high in countries where the legal system is flawed or corrupt and defendants may not have adequate legal representation or a fair trial.

Another concern is using the death penalty against vulnerable groups, such as minors or those with mental disabilities. The execution of such individuals is seen by many as a violation of their human rights, as they may not fully understand the nature of the crime they are accused of or the punishment they are facing.

Finally, there is concern about using the death penalty in a discriminatory manner, with certain groups, such as minorities and the poor, disproportionately represented on death row. This can be due to various factors, including bias among judges and juries and unequal access to legal representation.

Conclusion:

The use of the death penalty is a complex issue that raises several human rights concerns. While international standards and norms have emerged that call for the abolition of the death penalty, many countries continue to use capital punishment as a form of punishment for the most severe crimes. The ongoing debate over the use of the death penalty underscores the importance of continued engagement and dialogue among policymakers, human rights advocates, and other stakeholders as societies grapple with questions about the appropriate limits of state power and the nature of justice.

CHAPTER 4: THE DEATH PENALTY AND RACE

The relationship between race and the death penalty has long been a contentious issue in criminal justice systems worldwide. This chapter will examine the historical and contemporary relationship between race and the death penalty and how race can impact every stage of the capital punishment process.

Historical Context:

In the United States, the death penalty has been used disproportionately against people of colour, mainly Black and Hispanic. This is rooted in a long history of racial discrimination in the criminal justice system, from slavery and Jim Crow laws to contemporary issues such as racial profiling and bias among judges and juries.

Contemporary Issues:

Today, people of colour continue to be overrepresented on death row in the United States and other countries that use the death penalty. This is due to various factors, including racial bias in the criminal justice system, socioeconomic disparities that can make it more difficult for people of colour to access quality legal representation, and the over-policing of communities of colour.

One alarming trend in using the death penalty against people of colour is the high number of cases in which defendants are wrongfully convicted. Innocent people of colour have been sentenced to death based on false evidence, coerced confessions, and biased testimony from witnesses and experts.

Impact of Race:

The impact of race on the use of the death penalty can be seen at every stage of the process. For example, people of colour are more likely to be stopped, searched, and arrested than white individuals and are more likely to be charged with capital crimes. They are also less likely to have access to quality legal representation and more likely to face bias from judges and juries during their trials.

The impact of race can also be seen in the clemency process, which can determine whether a defendant's sentence is commuted from death to life in prison. Studies have shown that governors and pardon boards are less likely to grant clemency in cases involving people of colour, particularly Black defendants.

Conclusion:

The relationship between race and the death penalty is a complex and profoundly ingrained issue in criminal justice systems worldwide. While international standards and norms have emerged that call for the abolition of the death penalty, the overrepresentation of people of colour on death row underscores the need for continued engagement and dialogue among policymakers, human rights advocates, and other stakeholders as societies work to address the racial disparities that exist in their criminal justice systems.

CHAPTER 5:
ALTERNATIVES TO
THE DEATH PENALTY

The use of the death penalty as a form of punishment has been a highly contentious issue for centuries, with supporters and opponents arguing over its effectiveness as a deterrent, cost, and moral implications. In recent years, however, there has been a growing movement to abolish and replace the death penalty with alternative forms of punishment. This chapter will examine some of the alternative approaches proposed and implemented in different jurisdictions worldwide.

Life Imprisonment without Parole:

One of the most common alternatives to the death penalty is life imprisonment without the possibility of parole. This sentence provides severe punishment for the most heinous crimes while avoiding the risks associated with capital punishment, such as wrongful convictions and the risk of executing innocent people.

Restorative Justice:

Restorative justice is a process that aims to repair the harm caused by a crime by involving the victim, the offender, and the community in a dialogue about the offence and its impact. This approach prioritizes rehabilitation and reconciliation rather than punishment and has been successfully implemented in some jurisdictions as an alternative to the death penalty.

Community Service:

Community service is another alternative to the death penalty implemented in some countries. This approach requires offenders to perform a certain number of hours of community service, such as cleaning up public areas, assisting the elderly or disabled, or participating in educational programs. This approach is aimed at helping offenders understand the impact of their actions on their communities and providing them with an opportunity to make amends.

Mental Health Treatment:

In some cases, offenders who have committed serious crimes may suffer from mental health disorders contributing to their actions. Instead of imposing the death penalty, some jurisdictions have implemented mental health treatment programs as an alternative form of punishment. This approach seeks to address the crime's underlying causes and provide offenders with the treatment they need to recover and reintegrate into society.

Conclusion:

The debate over the death penalty will likely continue for many years. However, the alternatives outlined in this chapter provide evidence that there are viable alternatives to the death penalty that can effectively punish offenders while avoiding the moral and practical concerns associated with capital punishment. As societies address these complex issues, they must consider various alternatives and engage in open and informed dialogue with stakeholders, including victims, offenders, and human rights advocates.

CHAPTER 6:
CONCLUSION

The death penalty remains a deeply divisive issue in modern society, with proponents and opponents fiercely arguing their positions. As this book has explored, complex historical, social, and legal factors have shaped our understanding of capital punishment and its place in modern justice systems.

One of the key findings of this book is that the death penalty is not a simple or straightforward solution to crime and punishment. While it may provide a sense of closure or justice to some victims and their families, it raises crucial questions about the morality and effectiveness of state-sanctioned killing. Moreover, the death penalty is often marred by bias, discrimination, and procedural errors, which raise serious concerns about the fairness and impartiality of the criminal justice system.

In light of these concerns, this book has explored a range of alternatives to the death penalty that can effectively punish offenders while respecting human rights and due process. Life imprisonment without parole, restorative justice, community service, and mental health treatment are all examples of alternative approaches implemented in different jurisdictions worldwide.

Ultimately, deciding to retain or abolish the death penalty is a matter for individual societies and governments to decide.

However, it is crucial that any decision on this matter is based on a comprehensive and informed understanding of the issues at stake and considers the perspectives of all stakeholders, including victims, offenders, and human rights advocates. The ongoing debate over the death penalty reflects the complexities of modern justice systems and the constant search for a fair and practical approach to punishment and rehabilitation.

Hopefully, this book has contributed to this ongoing discussion and provided readers with a deeper understanding of the history, arguments, and alternatives surrounding the death penalty. By continuing to engage in open and informed dialogue, we can work towards a more just and humane criminal justice system that reflects our shared values and aspirations.

Furthermore, it is essential to acknowledge that the debate over the death penalty is not limited to legal and moral arguments alone. The death penalty also has significant social, economic, and political implications, which must be considered when considering its use. For example, the death penalty is often used as a tool of political control or propaganda in authoritarian regimes, where it is used to silence dissent or intimidate opposition groups. In such cases, the death penalty is not merely a legal issue but a fundamental challenge to democracy, human rights, and the rule of law.

Similarly, using the death penalty can have significant economic costs, both in terms of the financial resources required to implement it and the broader economic and social consequences of capital punishment. For example, the death penalty can lead to lengthy and costly legal proceedings, diverting resources from other social and economic development areas. Additionally, the death penalty can harm international trade and investment, as countries and companies are increasingly unwilling to do business with jurisdictions that practice capital punishment.

Given these complexities, it is clear that the decision to retain or abolish the death penalty must be based on a comprehensive and nuanced understanding of the issues involved. This requires ongoing dialogue and engagement with all stakeholders, including victims, offenders, human rights advocates, and the broader community. We can build a more just, fair, and humane criminal justice system that reflects our shared values and aspirations by working together to address these complex issues.

BIBLIOGRAPHY

Books:

- Banner, S. (2002). The Death Penalty: An American History. Harvard University Press.
- Bedau, H. A., & Cassell, P. G. (Eds.). (2018). Debating the Death Penalty: Should America Have Capital Punishment? Oxford University Press.
- Bohm, R. M. (2015). DeathQuest: An Introduction to the Theory and Practice of Capital Punishment in the United States. Routledge.
- Liebman, J. S., & Clarke, P. B. (2013). The Fallibility of the Death Penalty: Litigating Malfeasance, Convicting the Innocent, and Uncovering the Facts. Columbia University Press.
- Radelet, M. L., & Borg, M. J. (2009). The History and Politics of the Death Penalty: A Global Perspective. Palgrave Macmillan.

Journal Articles:

- Baumgartner, F. R., De Boef, S. L., & Boydstun, A. E. (2010). The Decline of the Death Penalty and the Discovery of Innocence. The Journal of Criminal Law and Criminology, 100(4), 1249-1286.
- Donohue, J. J., & Wolfers, J. (2006). The Death Penalty: No Evidence for Deterrence. National Bureau of Economic Research, Working Paper No. 11982.
- Garland, D. (2010). The Culture of Control: Crime and Social Order in Contemporary Society. Oxford University Press.
- Hood, R. (2015). The Death Penalty in Decline: From Error-

Correction to Risk Management. Annual Review of Law and Social Science, 11, 281-301.

- Steiker, C. S., & Steiker, J. M. (2010). Sober Second Thoughts: Reflections on Two Decades of Constitutional Regulation of Capital Punishment. Annual Review of Law and Social Science, 6, 85-109.

Reports:

- Amnesty International. (2021). Death Sentences and Executions 2020. Amnesty International.
- Death Penalty Information Center. (2021). The Death Penalty in 2020: Year End Report. Death Penalty Information Center.
- United Nations General Assembly. (2007). Moratorium on the use of the death penalty (A/RES/62/149). United Nations General Assembly.

Websites:

- The Innocence Project. (n.d.). Retrieved from https://www.innocenceproject.org/
- National Coalition to Abolish the Death Penalty. (n.d.). Retrieved from https://deathpenalty.org/
- ProDeathPenalty.com. (n.d.). Retrieved from http://www.prodeathpenalty.com/

EPILOGUE

As we come to the end of this book, it is essential to reflect on what we have learned about the death penalty and its place in modern society. We have seen that this is a complex and multifaceted issue with no easy answers.

While the death penalty has been used as a legal punishment for centuries, it remains a controversial and divisive topic. There are arguments for and against its use, and broader social, political, and cultural factors often shape these arguments.

We have seen that the death penalty has a complicated history and that its use has been linked to race, class, and inequality issues. Moreover, there are serious concerns about the fairness and accuracy of the criminal justice system and the potential for wrongful convictions and executions.

At the same time, proponents of the death penalty argue that it is a necessary measure of justice and deterrence and serves as a warning to potential criminals. They say that certain crimes are so heinous that the death penalty is the only appropriate punishment.

Ultimately, the debate over the death penalty reflects broader debates about justice, morality, and human rights. As we move forward, it is essential to continue to engage in thoughtful and informed discussions about this critical issue and to work towards creating a criminal justice system that is fair and equitable for all.

In conclusion, I hope this book has provided a deeper

understanding of the complexities and controversies surrounding the death penalty and has inspired continued debate and discussion on this critical topic.

AFTERWORD

The death penalty remains one of modern society's most controversial and polarizing issues. While some countries have abolished capital punishment, others continue to use it as a legal punishment for certain crimes. This book aims to critically examine the death penalty, exploring its history, arguments for and against it, its impact on human rights and race, and alternatives to its use.

Throughout this book, we have seen that the death penalty has flaws and controversies. There have been cases of wrongful convictions and executions and concerns about its effectiveness as a deterrent to crime. Moreover, the use of the death penalty has been linked to race and socioeconomic status, highlighting inequality and bias in the criminal justice system.

Nevertheless, the debate over the death penalty continues, with proponents arguing for its use as a necessary measure of justice and deterrence. In contrast, opponents argue for its abolition on the grounds of morality and human rights. This is a complex and nuanced issue with no easy answers.

As we move forward, we must continue engaging in thoughtful and informed discussions about the death penalty and its place in our society. By examining its history and impact, we can work towards creating a criminal justice system that is fair and equitable for all.

ACKNOWLEDGEMENT

Writing a book is never a solitary endeavour; this one was no exception. I want to express my sincere gratitude to everyone who supported me in this project.

Firstly, I would like to thank my family for their unwavering support and encouragement. Their love and understanding gave me the strength and motivation to see this project through.

I would also like to thank my colleagues and friends for their valuable insights and feedback, which helped shape this book into its final form. Your encouragement and support were instrumental in keeping me focused and inspired.

I want to acknowledge the authors of the many books, articles, and other sources referenced in this book. Their scholarship and research gave me the knowledge and understanding necessary to write this book.

Finally, I would like to thank the readers of this book for their interest in this vital topic. I hope this book will contribute to a greater understanding of the death penalty's complexities and controversies and inspire continued debate and discussion on this critical issue.

ABOUT THE AUTHOR

Muhammad Khalid Aziz Bari

Muhammad Khalid Aziz Bari is a Lawyer, Entrepreneur, YouTuber, Writer, Public Speaker, Traveller, and Nature Lover. He has an LLM from Bahria University Islamabad and is the Founder & CEO of Al-Khalid Law Firm, the fastest-growing law firm in Pakistan. The firm provides services in various fields of law, such as Civil, Criminal,  Family, Corporate, Banking, Income Tax, Sales Tax, Cybercrimes, Immigration, Visas, and more, serving clients worldwide. He is also the Managing Director of Free Legal Services (NGO), which aids in providing legal assistance to needy persons. Khalid Bari is the President of the Faisalabad Young Lawyers Forum (FYLF), where he strives to bring positive change to society, the legal fraternity, and the world. His passion for nature and sustainable practices is evident in his work, making him a reliable advocate committed to making a difference.

BOOKS BY THIS AUTHOR

Indigenous Rights And Land Stewardship: Discuss The Importance Of Indigenous Knowledge, Traditional Practices, And Land Rights In Environmental Conservation And Sustainable Resource Management

"Indigenous Rights and Land Stewardship: Discuss the Importance of Indigenous Knowledge, Traditional Practices, and Land Rights in Environmental Conservation and Sustainable Resource Management" is a groundbreaking exploration of Indigenous communities' critical role in environmental conservation and sustainable resource management.

Drawing on extensive research, firsthand interviews, and deep engagement with Indigenous perspectives, this book delves into the profound wisdom, historical injustices, and ongoing struggles Indigenous Peoples face worldwide. It examines the intricate connection between Indigenous knowledge, traditional practices, and the preservation of land, culture, and heritage.

Through vivid storytelling and thought-provoking analysis, the authors shed light on the indispensable contributions of Indigenous Peoples to our understanding of ecosystems, biodiversity, and the delicate balance between human communities and the natural world. They unveil the profound intergenerational stewardship embedded in Indigenous cultures, highlighting how traditional ecological knowledge is vital to sustainable resource management and environmental resilience.

The chapters of this book explore a wide range of topics, including the wisdom of the ancestors, historical injustices and their impact on Indigenous Peoples, the significance of land rights and sovereignty, the preservation and revitalization of Indigenous knowledge, and the emergence of Indigenous guardianship as a powerful force for protecting sacred lands and waters.

Moreover, this book addresses the challenges and opportunities that lie ahead, including the urgent need to address climate change, industrial development, and social inequalities. It calls for collaboration, solidarity, and recognizing Indigenous rights as essential in pursuing environmental justice.

Through its comprehensive and thought-provoking analysis, this book invites readers to broaden their perspectives, challenge preconceptions, and embrace a more inclusive and sustainable approach to environmental conservation. It provides a roadmap for policymakers, activists, scholars, and individuals passionate about creating a future that respects and integrates Indigenous knowledge, upholds land rights, and promotes environmental harmony.

"Indigenous Rights and Land Stewardship" is a compelling testament to the resilience, wisdom, and aspirations of Indigenous Peoples. It inspires us to engage in meaningful dialogue, fosters a deeper understanding of environmental justice, and calls us to action in support of Indigenous rights and the protection of our planet for generations to come.

Join us on this transformative journey and discover the profound importance of Indigenous knowledge, traditional practices, and land rights in environmental conservation and sustainable resource management.

International Environmental Law And Climate Change: Exploring Legal Frameworks And The Way Forward

This book provides an in-depth exploration of the legal frameworks governing international environmental law and climate change. It covers the scientific consensus on climate change, the role of human activities in driving climate change, and the potential consequences of global warming. The book examines existing legal frameworks, such as the United Nations Framework Convention on Climate Change and the Paris Agreement, and explores the potential for legal mechanisms to facilitate effective climate action. It also discusses the challenges and opportunities for effective climate action, including the potential for innovative legal mechanisms and the promotion of sustainable development and equitable outcomes. Overall, the book aims to provide a comprehensive understanding of the legal dimensions of climate change and the way forward for effective climate action.

Seven Habits Of Successful Lawyers

"Seven Habits of Successful Lawyers" is a practical and insightful guide for lawyers who want to succeed in their careers. Drawing on the wisdom and experience of successful lawyers, this book identifies seven essential habits for building a thriving legal practice.

Each chapter is devoted to one of these habits and provides in-depth explanations, real-world examples, and practical strategies for developing and applying the habit in your practice.

This book is designed to be accessible and engaging for lawyers at all stages of their careers, from law students and young associates to seasoned partners and solo practitioners. The habits outlined in this book are not just theoretical concepts but are based on the real-world experiences of successful lawyers who have honed these habits over years of practice.

Whether you are looking to advance in your current role, build a successful solo practice, or make a career transition, "Seven Habits of Successful Lawyers" provides a roadmap for achieving your goals and making a meaningful impact in the lives of your clients and colleagues.

Natural Resources Law: Managing Conflicts Between Resource Extraction And Conservation

"Natural Resources Law: Managing Conflicts Between Resource Extraction and Conservation" is a comprehensive guide that explores the complex and often contentious relationship between resource extraction and conservation. The book provides a detailed overview of the legal and policy frameworks that govern natural resource management, as well as the various types of natural resources that are subject to extraction and conservation. The book examines the key issues and challenges associated with managing conflicts between resource extraction and conservation, including the competing interests and values at play, the economic and environmental impacts of extraction and conservation, and the role of stakeholders in decision-making processes. The authors also provide a range of case studies that illustrate the real-world complexities of natural resource management and the various strategies that can be used to manage conflicts.

The book concludes with a discussion of the future directions of natural resources law, including emerging trends, challenges, and opportunities for innovation and collaboration. Throughout the book, the authors emphasize the importance of balancing the economic benefits of resource extraction with the need for environmental protection and sustainable development.

This book is an essential resource for anyone interested in natural resources law and policy, including scholars, policymakers, practitioners, and students. It provides a comprehensive and accessible overview of the key issues and challenges associated with managing conflicts between resource extraction and conservation, and offers practical strategies for promoting sustainable and equitable resource management.

Environmental Justice: Analyzing Legal

Approaches To Addressing Injustice In Environmental Decision-Making

"Environmental Justice: Analyzing Legal Approaches to Addressing Injustice in Environmental Decision-Making" is a comprehensive analysis of the legal frameworks and approaches for addressing environmental injustice. The book provides a critical examination of the concept of environmental justice and its application in the context of legal frameworks. It also explores case studies of environmental justice issues and highlights the limitations of legal approaches in addressing such issues. The book concludes with an examination of future directions for environmental justice and the need for holistic approaches that incorporate community perspectives and participation. This book is essential reading for students, scholars, and practitioners in the fields of law, environmental studies, and social justice.

Environmental Ethics And The Law: Examining The Relationship Between Human Values And Legal Regulations

"Environmental Ethics and the Law: Examining the Relationship Between Human Values and Legal Regulations" is a comprehensive exploration of the intersection of environmental ethics and law. This book provides an in-depth analysis of the ways in which human values shape environmental laws and policies, as well as how the legal system can reflect and shape ethical considerations regarding the environment. The book is organised into several sections, including an introduction to environmental ethics and law, an exploration of the relationship between these two fields, an examination of human values and their impact on environmental policy, and a discussion of environmental ethics in practice. Each section is grounded in theoretical and practical perspectives, providing readers with a thorough understanding of the complex issues at the heart of the intersection of environmental ethics and the law. Throughout the book, readers will be presented with real-world case studies illustrating the key concepts and themes discussed. These case studies cover a range of environmental issues, from climate change and pollution to wildlife conservation and sustainable development. Through these examples, readers will understand the practical implications of environmental ethics and law in today's world. This book is an essential resource for students, scholars, policymakers, and anyone interested in understanding the relationship between environmental ethics and the law. It offers a thoughtful and nuanced perspective on a critical issue facing our society today and provides insights into how we can work towards a more sustainable and just future.

The Impact Of Environmental Law On Business Practices

This book explores the intersection of environmental law and business practices. As society becomes more aware of the impacts of environmental issues such as climate change, pollution, and biodiversity loss, environmental law has evolved to address these challenges. This book provides a comprehensive overview of the evolution of environmental law, its impact on business practices, and the benefits and challenges of environmental regulation.

The book delves into the role of corporate social responsibility and the potential future trends in environmental law and business practices. It also examines the benefits of complying with environmental regulations and incorporating sustainability practices in business operations.

The book emphasizes the importance of collaboration and stakeholder engagement in addressing environmental issues. Governments, businesses, civil society, and other stakeholders must work together to promote sustainable development and protect the environment.

Overall, this book is a valuable resource for students, researchers, policymakers, and practitioners interested in understanding the relationship between environmental law and business practices and the role of sustainability in shaping the future of business operations.

www.ingramcontent.com/pod-product-compliance
Lightning Source LLC
Chambersburg PA
CBHW070858220526
45466CB00005B/2042